I0617552

THE WAITING ROOM II
and The Saved Thief

Two Plays In One

ADEOLA OYEKOLA

The Waiting Room II and The Saved Thief
All Rights Reserved.
Copyright 2024 by Adeola Oyekola

This is a work of fiction. The events and characters described herein are imaginary and are not intended to refer to specific places or living persons. The opinions expressed in this manuscript are solely the opinions of the author and do not represent the opinions or thoughts of the publisher. The author has represented and warranted full ownership and/or legal right to publish all the materials in this book.

This book may not be reproduced, transmitted, or stored in whole or in part by any means, including graphic, electronic, or mechanical without the express written consent of the publisher except incase of brief quotations embodied in critical articles and reviews.

First Printing, 2024

OLABOOKS INTERNATIONAL
MY BOOK • MY PASSION

http://www.olabooksinternationalselfpub.com

Cover photo@2023 www.shutterstock.com. Used with permission.
ISBN: 978-1-7363889-9-0 (eBook)
ISBN: 979-8-9897213-0-6 (Paperback)

PRINTED IN THE UNITED STATES OF AMERICA

CONTENTS

THE WAITING ROOM II

A One-Act Play

CAST

Narrator 1: An elderly male character who narrates the story

Narrator 2: An elderly male character who co-narrates the story

Abraham: An elderly handsome man

Sarah: A beautiful elderly woman

Haggai: A beautiful young maid

Ishmael: A rude teenage boy

Isaac: A two-year-old who gets a lot of attention from his parents

Dance Troupe: Performing arts group

Other Family Members: Some male and female characters from Abraham's household

God: A man dressed like a Yoruba king sitting on a throne

This Play is written to show cultural diversity. You may explore any culture of your choice as directed by the director.

Scene One

[Opens with a choreographed dance to a Yoruba song. The dancers dance vigorously and flawlessly, with excitement and pleasure. As they leave the stage joyfully and the audience claps, the narrators enter, trying to imitate the dancers. They appreciate the dancers and introduce the audience to the story.]

NARRATOR 1
What a beautiful dance -

NARRATOR 2
By beautiful dancers!

NARRATOR 1
How I wish we would showcase our culture every day and everywhere.

NARRATOR 2
I am with you on that. We should be proud of what we have at all times. I mean, our traditional attires, culture, language, ethics, artistry, and more are so wonderful.

NARRATOR 1
Do you know what I love so much about our use of language?

NARRATOR 2
What?

NARRATOR 1

"Òwe àti àsàyàn òrò," proverbs and idioms.

NARRATOR 2

Hmm...

NARRATOR 1

"Tí etí kò bá gbó yìnkìn, inú kí í bàjé".

NARRATOR 2

[Thoughtfully]

Hmm... meaning, you will not be sad if you do not hear or listen to unpleasant stories.

NARRATOR 1

You did well, my brother. Most times, translations do not do justice to the meaning of rich word usage in our languages.

NARRATOR 2

So, what is the story today? Because I know you; you didn't just use that proverb for no reason.

NARRATOR 1

[Sighs]

I was reading the story of Isaac, and I got stuck on some convincing developments surrounding his upbringing and family. You know that Abraham had a child from Haggai named Ishmael, right?

NARRATOR 2
Yes.

NARRATOR 1
Okay, was there any reason you think the two boys didn't grow up together in their father's house?

NARRATOR 2
Haba, we all know Sarah sent Ishmael away out of jealousy. She didn't want Ishmael to share in Isaac's inheritance.

NARRATOR 1
Maybe. But what about Ishmael's attitude?

NARRATOR 2
What about it?

[In the background, we hear drums and song for a naming ceremony. The narrators communicate non-verbally, demonstrating holding a baby, and they danced off the stage.]

[CURTAIN]

SCENE TWO

[A birthday party for Isaac. He has just turned two. A modern, blue-themed two-year-old party, colorful and beautiful. Isaac, along with his mother, father, Ishmael, and other family members, are dressed in African attire. Isaac is getting ready to cut his beautifully decorated cake. Abraham is a black, medium height, handsome, elderly man with curly hair and a clean attractive look. His deep-set black eyes and bushy eyebrows are more noticeable because of his overflowing joy on this occasion. Sarah is an outstanding beauty, even in her old age. Her dark brown skin radiates, enhancing her happy demeanor. She is just the right fit for Abraham. She carries herself with glee and glamor fit for a queen.]

SARAH
Isaac, it's time to cut your cake. Let me put your hat right.

[She adjusts his hat and straightens his top. Ishmael, a defiant 14-year-old, snickers. Sarah looks in his direction, and he quickly looks away.]

SARAH
Photographer, please capture good pictures for my one and only Isaac.

PHOTOGRAPHER
I will, madam.

SARAH
Stand upright, okay, smile...

PHOTOGRAPHER
[Politely]
Please, Madam Sarah, let me do my job.

SARAH
Oh, I just want my son to look good.

PHOTOGRAPHER
Okay, Isaac, look at me.

[He takes several shots.]

SARAH
[Smiling, proud, singing]
Happy birthday to you...

[She sings the song, and everyone but Ishmael sings along. Ishmael looks on in disdain, his horrible gaze on Isaac. While Sarah observes Ishmael's disposition, Abraham sings along obliviously and wishes his son well. The song ends.]

ABRAHAM
Sarah, the guests will soon arrive; is food ready?

SARAH
Yes, the servants have killed two fat cows, and the women have cooked.

ABRAHAM
[Nodding with pride]
What about chicken and the rest of the food?

SARAH
We have prepared 50 chickens, two big bags of rice, several pots of vegetable soup, uncountable mortars of pounded yam, my husband. We have fried rice, jollof rice, porridge, and many more dishes.

ABRAHAM
That's exactly what I was waiting to hear. I think I hear my guests coming in, I shall attend to them.

SARAH
[To Abraham]
And I will be with you shortly, my husband.
[Talking to the other family members present]
Indeed, today is a great day in our family. So I want you to make every guest welcome. We have plenty to eat and give away. Let everyone be happy…

[Ishmael snickers again. This time Sarah gives him a knowing look.]

SARAH
…And enjoy.

They exit the stage dancing.

[CURTAIN]

SCENE THREE

[Narrators are sitting in an eatery, eating pounded yam and vegetable soup.]

NARRATOR 1
[Smacking lips]
This is the best food I have eaten in about a month.

NARRATOR 2
I must agree, the food is good. But for me, not the best I have eaten all month.

NARRATOR 1
Stop lying; who would cook such a good meal for you?

[Narrator 1 licks his lips.]

NARRATOR 2
Can you stop eating so noisily? I really can tell you have not had a good meal in a long while.

NARRATOR 1
When I see a good meal, I do justice to it with my five senses.

[Narrator 1 rolls up a mound of swallow, throws it up and catches it. He delightfully dips it in the soup, scoops it up, and swallows gracefully.]

NARRATOR 1

I know you have not had a good meal like this one in a long time.

[Narrator 2 eats quietly with a fork.]

NARRATOR 2

Why are you so sure?

NARRATOR 1

You don't cook.

NARRATOR 2

So? I can pay for what I want to eat, I don't have to cook.

NARRATOR 1

Yes, and you are acting too sophisticated. You can be free, you know, you can feel at home with me. The best way to enjoy our local food is to eat with your fingers ...

NARRATOR 2

You want me to lick my fingers like you do with yours? Yuck!

NARRATOR 1

I might have overdone it a little, but I only because I think I can be free around you. I can choose to be me, unburden my mind, play around, loosen up, and have the best of times. You can do that with me too. Life is sweeter when you have people who understand and appreciate you rather than judge you.

NARRATOR 2

Why do I get the feeling that has something to do with the story you're telling me?

NARRATOR 1

Because it does. Why do you think Ishmael was trying to belittle Isaac?

NARRATOR 2

He was probably jealous of him.

NARRATOR 1

Jealous? Why?

NARRATOR 2

Ishmael was the only child for a while. I mean, his mom celebrated him and even used him to taunt Sarah. But then, suddenly, a new child came from nowhere to take his place. He had to be jealous.

NARRATOR 1

But where there is love, peace, and harmony, there should be no jealousy. We should all be free and endure one another in love. If there were any signs of jealousy, Haggai should have knocked it out of Ishmael. But what we see is Ishmael taking after his mother. Remember, like you said, Haggai mocked Sarah when she had Ishmael.

NARRATOR 2

That is so true!

[He drops his fork and picks up a piece of meat with his fingers and takes a bite. He nods his head in approval.]

NARRATOR 2
So good...tastes better with my hands.

[They both laugh.]

NARRATOR 1
Let's be natural and real.

NARRATOR 2
Yes, brother. You know, even if Sarah was not a perfect mistress to Haggai, she trusted Haggai with her family. Her intention was for Haggai to represent her well, but the reverse was the case.

NARRATOR 1
The Yoruba people would say, "igi gogoro má gún mi lójú àtòkèèrè láá tí n wòó".

NARRATOR 2
That one is too much for me. What does it mean?

NARRATOR 1
Ask Google.

NARRATOR 2
[Washing and wiping his hands]
Why not just tell me? Why ask Google? You know the answer, just tell me.

[Narrator 1 shakes his head and points to the phone.]

NARRATOR 2
Don't tell me, I will ask.

[Narrator 2 starts to type on his phone.]

NARRATOR 2
How do you spell the words?

NARRATOR 1
Give me the phone.

[He takes the phone and says the words as he types.]

NARRATOR 1
You go to google translate, find Yoruba and type in-
"igi... go... goro... má... gún... mi... lójú... àtò... kèèrè... láá...
tí... n... wòó".... translation... It's loading... What?

NARRATOR 2
What is it?

NARRATOR 1
Ha, Google will not kill me o! [laughs out loud and for a little while]

NARRATOR 2
Is the proverb that funny? Let me see.
[Trying to take the phone from him]

NARRATOR 1
[Tries to contain his laughter]
Wait, I'll read it to you.

[He clears his throat and starts to read.]

NARRATOR 1
The proverb is, "igi gogoro mágún mi lójú àtòkèèrè láá tí n wòó".
Here's Google's translation: "Don't let the tall tree stab me in the eyes of the people I'm looking at."

NARRATOR 2
Wha…what? I don't get it.

NARRATOR 1
You can't get it, 'cos that's not the meaning. Let me tell you the literal meaning: "For a stick from a tall tree not to injure your eyes, you have to look from afar". Or take for instance, someone is holding a long stick or stem, you don't want to move too close so your eyes don't get into an accident with it.

NARRATOR 2
[Thinks briefly]
Ooh…in essence, proper planning prevents poor result.

NARRATOR 1
Yes, and you can also say, prevention is better than cure.

NARRATOR 1

Exactly. So, Sarah saw then what the household would become with Ishmael as a member... loveless and terrifying for Isaac, because a bully was already in place.

NARRATOR 2

Hmm...

NARRATOR 1

So, she took a step...

[Narrator 1 pours water in both their cups and they begin to drink as the curtain closes on them.]

SCENE FOUR

Abraham and Sarah are in Abraham's room having a discussion. In the room there is a bed and two pillows, two lamp stands, one on each side of the bed, and a flower vase.

ABRAHAM
[Yawning]
What a beautiful, tiring day.

[He removes his cap and places it on the lamp stand.]

ABRAHAM
I must commend your effort, dear. That was a great party for our dear son, Isaac.

SARAH
Yes, I am so happy. I didn't know I still had the energy to dance so much.

ABRAHAM
You didn't dance as much as I did.

SARAH
Really? We can start again, you know.

[She begins to show a dance step.]

ABRAHAM
No, no, no ... I give up. You wouldn't believe how tired I am.

SARAH
That's what I thought.
[She smiles in victory.]

ABRAHAM
[Yawning]
These old bones need some rest.

[He sits and leans on a pillow]

SARAH
Just a minute, darling, before you doze off.

ABRAHAM
Can it wait till tomorrow?

SARAH
The earlier the better.

ABRAHAM
[In between a yawn and a stretch]
Okay, my darling Sarah, what is it?

SARAH
Ishmael.

[Abraham reacts to Sarah's words with a sharp and questioning look]

SARAH
[Frowns]
Don't look at me like that. Don't tell me you didn't see how he sneered at Isaac today.

ABRAHAM
When? How?

SARAH
At the party. He was sneering and jeering and trying to belittle me and my precious Isaac. I saw him, and it was not the first time he would do something like that. You were there, I don't know why you didn't see all of these things happening. I wouldn't be lying about him. If he didn't do it, I wouldn't have said he did.

ABRAHAM
I never said you were lying, all I said was I didn't see it.

SARAH
Just because you didn't see it doesn't mean it didn't happen.

ABRAHAM
I didn't say it didn't happen. You know what, I believe you. What do you want us to do about it?

SARAH

If this behavior should continue, we would not be raising happy children. There would be disunity in this household.

ABRAHAM

Okay. What should we do about it?

SARAH

Our precious Isaac would be at the receiving end because he is the youngest.

ABRAHAM

Okay...

SARAH

Ishmael is the son of my maid, Haggai. You are a witness to how she suddenly became rude and uncontrollable ever since she had her son. Now the son has taken after his mother with his recent behavior. They both forget that I made them who they are today, and that this is my home that I chose to share with them. And they dared to mock me and my son?

ABRAHAM

[Getting impatient]

I know, Sarah, what do you want me to do?

SARAH

Send them away! Mother and son away!

ABRAHAM

What? Send my son away?

SARAH

Yes, send him away. You now have Isaac. You would never have had Ishmael if I didn't push you toward her. That boy has no inheritance here. I will never, ever allow the son of that woman to share in Isaac's inheritance. Never!

[Her voice echoes as the curtains are drawn.]

SCENE FIVE

[Haggai enters looking for Ishmael. He is standing by himself sulking in a corner of what is left of Isaac's party room.]

HAGGAI
Ishmael, I've looked everywhere for you. Why are you still here?

ISHMAEL
[No response]

HAGGAI
My son, what's wrong with you, you don't look happy?

ISHMAEL
I did everything you asked me to do, Mother, but nothing worked. His mother had back up plans.

HAGGAI
What exactly did you do?

ISHMAEL
I tried to shoot at Isaac with a catapult, but there was a guard in the yard watching him play who saw me and sent me away. I sneaked into the mother's room and took his favorite outfit; I burned it in the yard. When he came out for the party, he had on a more befitting one. I even set a trap for the mother to trip and fall, but she went another way. I am so angry, Mother.

HAGGAI

We'll keep on trying to make their lives miserable, son. There are many more tricks we can use. We just need to keep tabs on them.

ISHMAEL

But, Mother, they still had the party, and they are all very happy. Father had never celebrated me like that before. Why, am I not his son?

HAGGAI

Of course, you are. You are his first son. Sarah is just trying to make you less noticeable. That is why we must continue to fight her and her son until you get your rightful place as the first son of this family. The inheritance in it is huge for you.

ISHMAEL

Ok, Mother. What's the next step.

Haggai

"Bí iná kò bá tán láso èjè kìí tán léè káná" If lice continue to remain in one's clothes, one's fingernails will have to keep getting stained with blood.

ISHMAEL

What does that mean, Mother?

HAGGAI

There is a traditional clothing that can harbor lice if allowed. And the lice will live like a parasite in the clothing just like it would in the human hair. The ancient way to kill lice is to find them one after the other and crush them. In our case, Sarah and Isaac are the lice in our clothing and we must be persistent in making sure you get your rightful place as the first son of Abraham.

ISHMAEL
Hmm, now I understand. We need to crush them [snapping his fingers] as many times as possible.

[We hear an eerie drumbeat. Haggai and Ishmael smile and begins to dance to the drums. After a while, they dance off stage]

[CURTAIN]

Scene Six

[Abraham is pacing the room in his pajamas, talking to himself worriedly. He is oblivious of God sitting as a king on His throne, in a corner in the room. He hears God but does not see him.]

ABRAHAM
What is this thing that Sarah has started? How can I push my own son away? Send him away...to where?

[He stands still for a while, shakes his head, makes gestures and mutters inaudibly.]

ABRAHAM
I can't quite think of a solution. I am the head of my house and I say no to Sarah. This is incomprehensible; how can I send my son away? Jealousy, they say, is the root of all evil. Sarah has allowed her carnal mind to rule over her. I will be a man and do the right thing. Ishmael is going nowhere!

GOD
Yes, he is.

ABRAHAM
Yes, he is?

GOD
Why are you sad about your maid's son? Listen to Sarah and do what she has requested that you do.

Abraham's mouth is ajar, surprised. He looks around for the person speaking.

ABRAHAM
My God, is that you?

GOD
"For Isaac is the son through whom your descendants will be counted. But I will also make a nation of the descendants of Haggai's son, because he is your son, too."

ABRAHAM
[Kneels in reverence]
Thank you, my Lord. I will surely do what pleases you.

[He gets up and walks away briskly, muttering under his breath]

ABRAHAM
I will listen to Sarah and do her will.

[CURTAIN]

Scene Seven

[The narrators come back with vigorous dance steps set to African percussion. When the dance is over, they continue their discussion.]

NARRATOR 2

I tell you, you're no match for me any day. When it comes to dance steps, I always nail it.

NARRATOR 1

Really? Who announced you the winner?

NARRATOR 2

Myself. I know I dance better than you.

NARRATOR 1

Don't be quick to judge. I know I danced pretty well, too. We need another opinion.

NARRATOR 2

Aha… that's how I know I did better, your tone said it.

NARRATOR 1

What! You can't be too sure. Sometimes you think you are right because it is logical or because you are the authority to judge, but your opinion might still be wrong.

NARRATOR 2

Just like Sarah's idea was the right one.

NARRATOR 1

Yes. Oh, how I love Father Abraham and his humility. How many men would value their wife's opinion and meditate on it like Abraham did?

NARRATOR 2

Not too many. If I were in Abraham's shoes, I would tell Sarah point blank, "You must be crazy to think I would listen to you. What rubbish! Ishmael mocked you, so what? Correct him, even spank him, but send him out of the house for mockery? No."

NARRATOR 1

You can't question destiny.

NARRATOR 2

You may be right.

NARRATOR 1

The Yorubas would say, "Omo tí ekùn bí ẹkùn ni ò jo."

NARRATOR 2

Hmm… a lion's offspring will behave like a lion.

NARRATOR 1

Very true. Ishmael was another Haggai, a pain in the neck to Sarah.

NARRATOR 2

Who wants someone like that around them?

NARRATOR 1
No one. Or at least, not me.

NARRATOR 2
Not me either. The moment I find out who my enemy is, they're gone!

NARRATOR 1
Gone where?

NARRATOR 2
Anywhere but near me.

NARRATOR 1
What happened to keeping your friends close and your enemies closer?

NARRATOR 2
What did you just say? You will keep an enemy inside your home? "Rárá o". I subscribe to Madam Sarah's point of view: send your enemies away if you have the power to do so. Some principalities and powers can be dealt with physically. Just send them away, "lóbátán ."

NARRATOR 1
Yes, Abraham joined that school of thought immediately after he heard from God.

[We hear the drums again, but softly. The narrator begins a gentle dance towards the exit]

NARRATOR 1
It was emotional for him, but he did it.

NARRATOR 2
He better have!

[CURTAIN]

SCENE EIGHT

[Abraham in his well-furnished living room. He is pacing up and down, looking sad. There's a basket of food and a pitcher of water on the center table. He occasionally glances at those items and shakes his head. He has a peculiar way of hanging his head when in deep thought. While pacing, Haggai and Isaac walk in.]

HAGGAI
You sent for us.

ABRAHAM
[Sighing]
Yes, I did. Haggai...

HAGGAI
Yes, sir.

ABRAHAM
I hate to say this, but I have to do things right.

HAGGAI
Yes, sir.

ABRAHAM
You and Ishmael do not belong here.

HAGGAI
What do you mean, sir?

ABRAHAM
I mean that you must leave.

HAGGAI
Leave to where? What are you talking about?

ABRAHAM
Isaac and Ishmael cannot live together in the same house, so you both will have to leave.

HAGGAI
You keep saying we have to leave, but where can we go? Ishmael is your first son, the son you were waiting for that came just in time.

ABRAHAM
No. Ishmael is a blessed child of mine, but he is not Isaac. I waited for Isaac. Come here, Ishmael.

[Ishmael walks to his father and gives him a hug]

ABRAHAM
You will go with your mother. The Lord will keep and lead you in the way to go.

[Ishmael begins to cry]

[He turns to Haggai]

ABRAHAM

Here is food and water for the journey. God will always provide for you when you run out of supplies.

[Abraham lifts up the food basket and water and passes them over to Haggai and Ishmael. As they walk away, he looks really heartbroken.]

[CURTAIN]

SCENE NINE

[Narrator 1 and Narrator 2 enters doing a solemn dance to a solemn song. After a few steps, they stop the dance and start to talk.]

NARRATOR 2
I feel sorry for Abraham.

NARRATOR 1
Hmm, "Ìrònú dōrí àgbà kōdò".

NARRATOR 2
Huh, meaning "Thinking bowed the head of the elder" ...

[They both laugh hysterically.]

NARRATOR 1
[Still laughing]
You must be another Google ...

NARRATOR 2
Please, be serious.

NARRATOR 1
I should be telling you to be serious, you gave a funny interpretation.

NARRATOR 2
Why is it funny? I gave the literal meaning.

NARRATOR 1
Why did you laugh?

NARRATOR 2
Because you laughed.

NARRATOR 1
If that's how you want it, I'll just continue with the story.

NARRATOR 2
No, no, tell the real meaning now,
[Gesturing to the audience]
we want to know.

NARRATOR 1
"Ìrònú dōrí àgbà kōdò", meaning, "The elder's head is bowed in deep thought." [Demonstrating]

NARRATOR 2
Hmm... so true, Abraham was very sad.

NARRATOR 1
What father wouldn't be? Do you know what it means to be separated from one's child? And like Haggai rightly said, Ishmael came while Abraham and Sarah thought all hope was lost for them to have a child.

NARRATOR 2
But Ishmael was not the promised child.

NARRATOR 1

No, he wasn't. He was Sarah's idea that came into manifestation.

NARRATOR 2

How many of our ideas have materialized and ended up shooting us in the foot?

NARRATOR 1

That's a deep one. Decision-making has always been a tough one for me, just for the fear of making mistakes.

NARRATOR 2

Fear... the fear of...

[Narrator 1 sighs.]

NARRATOR 2

I think we should be logical, pray, listen, and follow directions as the Lord leads, but fear should not be a part of our decision process.

NARRATOR 1

I know, right?

NARRATOR 2

Grace, we all need grace.

NARRATOR 1

Yes, grace.

[They both mouth the word "grace" as they solemnly danced out of the stage.]

Scene Ten

[Haggai and Ishmael in the bush. Ishmael has a bottle of water around his neck, and Haggai is carrying a bag of food. They are walking and dragging their feet, tired.]

ISHMAEL
Mother.

HAGGAI
Yes, Ishmael, my son.

ISHMAEL
Can we take another break? I am tired and thirsty.

HAGGAI
Of course.
[Pointing]
There is a tree over there, we can sit under the shade for some time while we quench our thirst.

[They walk to the tree and sit under the tree. Ishmael puts the bottle of water in his mouth, but nothing comes out. He bursts into tears.]

ISHMAEL
I'm thirsty, I need some water.

[Haggai looks at him with pity.]

ISHMAEL

Mother, do you have any more bread?

HAGGAI

No. Please don't cry, darling, I will look around for food and water. Just lie down under this tree, I will be right back.

[Ishmael continues to cry softly. Haggai walks a few feet away, sits, and begins to sob.]

HAGGAI

I can't bear watching my son die of hunger. I know we will both die in this bush. No water, no food, what can a hopeless mother like me do?

[She cries. Ishmael cries. While crying, an angel appears and talks to her.]

ANGEL

There's no need to be afraid, Haggai. Go and lift up your son and continue to lead him. God has heard the voice of Ishmael crying. He will make him a great nation.

[Haggai nods in affirmation, then she hears water. She rushes back to her son, calling him excitedly.]

HAGGAI

Ishmael, Ishmael, let's go, I have found water!

[Ishmael and Haggai briskly walk off the stage.]

[CURTAIN]

Scene Eleven

[Narrators enter with a background of solemn song. When they reach the center og the stage, the songs fades away and they begin to talk.]

NARRATOR 2

I never thought Ishmael had a waiting room. We seem to always use his story negatively, but I must confess, he had at least one tough moment in his life, and God saw him through.

NARRATOR 1

Have you ever met a human being who never goes through hardship? It's not possible. Life is full of ups and downs no matter who you are.

NARRATOR 2

Imagine them all alone in the bush, how come a wild animal didn't get to them?

NARRATOR 1

God was watching over them.

NARRATOR 2

Hmm, interesting. That is kind of off, because Ishmael and Haggai were not nice to Sarah and Isaac. Shouldn't God show that he is on Sarah's side by punishing Ishmael and Haggai? God shouldn't be nice to them.

NARRATOR 1

You forget that God's promise is on Ishmael because he came from Abraham. God stands by His words, always. He never fails, He never changes.

NARRATOR 2

Hmm, is that why sometimes I wish some people would be struck down by fire and brimstone and it never happens!

NARRATOR 1

You see, you want someone to be struck down by fire and brimstone! If God should answer that prayer, how many people would be left on earth?

NARRATOR 2

As many as are righteous.

NARRATOR 1

Name one righteous person you know.

NARRATOR 2

Me, I am righteous.

NARRATOR 1

You?

NARRATOR 2

Yes, me. I can stand up for myself.

NARRATOR 1

You, who want to strike someone down with fire and brimstone, are righteous? Ha!

NARRATOR 2

Eh, some people are so wicked, you need to see the kind of atrocities they commit. I maintain, they should be struck down with fire and brimstone.

[Just then, it thunders. They both shake with fear.]

NARRATOR 1

Did you call down thunder too?

[It thunders again, and they scamper off the stage. Narrator 1 hurriedly returns to the stage.]

NARRATOR 1

I was saying...both Christians and non-Christians have sometimes in their lives when they're waiting for a change to come. Don't ever look down on anyone. While waiting for your miracle, have faith and be kind.

[It thunders again, and he runs off the stage dramatically. We hear the drums beating hysterically.]

THE END

THE SAVED THIEF

A One-Act Play

By

Adeola Oyekola

CAST

Clara: A young undergraduate who has just found a passion in writing

Victor: Clara's friend

Jack: A wayward friend of Victor's

Jesus: A middle aged modern day dressed Jesus

Police Officers: Uniformed men

Gritty Voice

Church members: A few people

Angel: A tall person dressed in white

SCENE ONE

[The curtain opens to reveal a group of people dispersing from church. They are mouthing their greetings, smiling and hugging one another, and walking away. Victor and Clara are also greeting one another and having a conversation loud enough for the audience to hear them.]

CLARA
Hello Victor!

VICTOR
Hi Clara! So good to see you.

CLARA
Same here. How are you and your baby sister?

VICTOR
We are doing very well, by His grace.

CLARA
We thank God.

VICTOR
And you?

CLARA
I'm okay, I can't complain.

VICTOR
It is well my sister. Life is full of difficulties, but we live assured that all will be well.

CLARA
[Sighing]
Thank you. That was refreshing.

VICTOR
You're always welcome.

CLARA
You know, Victor, the challenges I faced recently have helped me develop a skill I never knew I had.

VICTOR
Really? What skill is that?

[Clara looks around and notices that all the people behind them are gone.]

CLARA
It seems like everyone is gone. Do you have some time?

VICTOR
Sure.

CLARA
[Pointing to a bench outside the church]
Let's sit over there.

[Showing him her phone]
Look at this, Victor.

VICTOR
Is this a poem?

CLARA
Yes, it is.

VICTOR
This is good. Who wrote it?

CLARA
I did.

VICTOR
[Astonished]
Are you a poet now?

CLARA
[Proud]
You can say that again. That's what I do now. When I find myself alone, instead of brooding over the challenges I am facing, I just sit and write.

[She scrolls on her phone.]

CLARA
Now, let me show you this script I started writing. I think it might be good for Easter. Here it is.

[She shows him the script.]

[Victor reads for a while, stands up, looks at her and smiles.]

VICTOR
This is good. I mean, when can we rehearse this play?

CLARA
What? Is it that good?

VICTOR
Yes, it is.

CLARA
But it is not finished.

VICTOR
Then finish the story. In the meantime, I will talk to a few people who I know will be interested in acting in this with us.

CLARA
Okay, I'll work on this.

VICTOR
Good job Clara, I'll see you in school tomorrow.

[He walks away.]

CLARA
See you!

[When he is gone, she hugs herself fiercely.]

CLARA
Yes! I finally found a passion!

[CURTAIN]

Scene Two

[Clara is sitting at her desk in her lightly furnished bedroom. She is typing on her computer. She pauses as if thinking of what to write next, and then continues to type. Her phone rings and she picks it up.]

CLARA
Hello, Victor

VICTOR
Hi, Clara. You won't believe this.

CLARA
What?

VICTOR
I spoke to the Pastor about your play, and he will let us stage it on Easter Sunday.

CLARA
What Play are you talking about?

VICTOR
Are you serious now, Clara? The same Play you showed me. I read it, remember?

Clara
The same Play I did not finish writing.

VICTOR

You were going to finish it? What's wrong Clara? Don't tell me you're having a second thought.

CLARA

I don't know, Victor. I mean, I am here still struggling to finish writing this play and you already told the Pastor, what if I can't finish writing the Play? What if they don't like it? Moreso, it's only a playlet, nothing serious.

VICTOR

You've got cold feet. Clara, even if you're not confident about your story, be confident about the message it carries and the people it might bless. Plus, your story has a good evangelism theme. If God helped you start this, His grace will help you finish it. You need to believe more in yourself.

CLARA

Thank you, Victor. I'll try my best.

VICTOR

Now, that's Clara talking. Do you mean I'll get it by the end of day today?

CLARA

Tomorrow, That's the best I can do.

VICTOR

Ok, Clara, tomorrow. And one more thing.

CLARA
What?

VICTOR
I spoke to a few people who might be interested in acting in the play.

CLARA
Already?

VICTOR
Yes. We're all waiting for you.

CLARA
Alright, then, Victor. You need to get off this phone, so I finish writing.

VICTOR
Talk to you tomorrow, Clara. [Hangs up]

CLARA
[Sighs]
This better be good. She looks at her computer and continues to type.

[CURTAIN]

Scene Three

[Victor is walking back and forth on stage constantly, looking at his wristwatch and muttering under his breath, getting impatient. Clara's Play is about to be staged and Clara has not arrived.]

VICTOR
Where is she? Where is she?

[He mutters and paces. He walks to the side of the stage where he picks up his phone from his pocket and dials.]

CLARA'S VOICE
Hello?

VICTOR
[Whispering]
For goodness' sake, where are you?

CLARA'S VOICE
On the bus.

VICTOR
On the bus? I am not sure you are looking at the time. The play is about to start!

CLARA'S VOICE
Oh … are we even sure people are coming?

VICTOR
What do you mean if people are coming? They are here already!

[He gestures to the audience.]

CLARA'S VOICE
Oh... really? I wasn't sure...

VICTOR
How far away are you?

CLARA'S VOICE
Ten minutes.

VICTOR
Are you kidding me? The play begins in 15 minutes and you're...

[He sighs.]

VICTOR
Just get here in ten minutes.

[He hangs up, puts his phone away, and walks back to the middle of the stage. Victor faces the audience and clears his throat.]

VICTOR
Good evening, ladies and gentlemen. We are so glad you are here. The play you are about to watch today is about the saved thief in the Bible. We tried to blend the ancient and the present ages together

while we tell the biblical story. We hope our blend blesses you tremendously.

[He bows and the audience claps.]

[CURTAIN]

SCENE FOUR

[Clara and Victor enter as the curtain opens. They both stay at a side of the stage to remind each other of the first scene.]

CLARA

We're going on stage now, don't forget your lines. I will start the conversation and you just flow along.

VICTOR

Okay, I won't forget, I just glanced through. You go in, and I'll follow you at the count of three. Ready?

CLARA

Yes, ready. No, no, no wait. Let me take a deep breath…Now I'm ready. [Victor counts to three and Clara walks to the middle of the stage along with Victor. Clara starts preaching to Victor.]

CLARA

As I was saying, Victor, do you know we have many verses in the bible that foretell the coming of this Jesus that you are rejecting? Isaiah 53: 3 says, "humanity despised and rejected him, a man of suffering, and familiar with pain…

VICTOR

[Taking the quote from her and finishing it]
"… Like one from whom people hide their face, He was despised, and we held him in low esteem."

CLARA

So, you know the verse?

VICTOR

What do you think of me? I am a church boy. Don't tell me you believe the arrant nonsense they preach! It's all fables, man.

CLARA

You're a church boy and you think the Bible is arrant nonsense?

VICTOR

I know there is a God, okay? I just don't believe in Jesus, period!

CLARA

But why?

VICTOR

It makes no sense, the son of man, or the son of God? I don't know, it's just too much to believe.

CLARA

No, it's simple, just believe in Jesus. Have you listened to His teachings?

VICTOR

No, why should I?

CLARA

You need to hear him speak life into you -

[Victor's phone rings, interrupting her.]

VICTOR
I'll answer this, okay?
[Talking into his phone]
What's up, man? For real, Jack?
[Getting excited]
... and it's tonight? Sure, sure, count me in ... I'll be on my way ...

CLARA
You still hang out with Jack?

VICTOR
What do you mean, that's my homie.

CLARA
But I always tell you ...

VICTOR
Always tell me what? Who do you think you are? My mother or something?

[He walks away, leaving Clara feeling embarrassed.]

CLARA
[Sighing]
I only tried to help, Victor! And I hope you're safe out there with ... Jack. Jack is not the best person to hang out with. [Frustrated. Sighs.] I'll call Jack, I should still have his number.

[She pulls out her phone and call Jack. The phone rings. Jack's voice responds to the call]

JACK'S VOICE
Yes?

CLARA
This is Clara

JACK'S VOICE
I know

CLARA
Did you just call Victor?

JACK'S VOICE
Yes, I did. What's your problem with that?

CLARA
I only hope you invited him to-

JACK'S VOICE
Church. That's where I invited him to.

CLARA
Are you mocking me?

Jack's Voice
[Sarcastic]
And why will I be mocking you? Isn't that where you invite everyone to?

[Getting serious]
Why do you still have my number, Clara? You should have deleted it a long time ago. Don't you ever give up?

CLARA
But-

JACK'S VOICE
No buts, Clara, have a great day [Ends the call]

CLARA
Jack? Jack...

[CURTAIN]

SCENE FIVE

[Jesus is dressed in jeans and a top matched with sneakers. He sits by a brook reading and meditating on his bible. Clara walks in looking sorrowful. Clara sits quietly beside Him. Jesus turns to look at her. She does not say anything; He says nothing. Tears roll down her eyes. Jesus looks at her with empathy.]

CLARA

The world is full of sorrow and dishonesty. Nothing brings satisfaction. I try, Lord. You know I try very hard to do well and find fulfillment in my ministry. It's not forthcoming. Why do I preach to people just to have them throw it back in my face? I just want to quit doing the right thing. If you can't beat them, then join them.

JESUS

Do not let your heart be troubled. You believe in God; believe also in me. My Father's house has many rooms; if that were not so, would I have told you I am going there to prepare a place for you? And if I prepare a place for you, I will come back and take you to be with me, that you also may be where I am. You know the way to the place where I am going.

CLARA

I know the way?

JESUS

I am the way and the truth and the life. No one comes to the Father except through me.

CLARA

Hmm…Do you think if I keep trying, I can win Victor for the kingdom?

[Jesus stands up and begin to walk away.]

JESUS

I am the way, the truth, and the life.

[Clara stands and follows him.]

CLARA

I mean…

Scene Six

[Jack and Victor are on the run with smuggled goods.]

JACK
Come on, Victor!

VICTOR
I'm doing my best, Jack, the bag is heavy.

[Police Officer 1 clears his throat from behind them. Jack and Victor try to run away but run into a second officer.]

POLICE OFFICER 2
Stop right there!

JACK
But why?

POLICE OFFICER 2
You are under arrest for breaking into your neighbor's house and stealing from them.

[Officers handcuff them.]

VICTOR
Take it easy, officer.

POLICE OFFICER 1

You have the right to remain silent. Anything you say will be used against you in the court of law.

JACK

We broke into a home... so what? Everyone does it. What's the big deal?

POLICE OFFICER 2

The big deal is you gently walk into the police car with me. You are going with us to the station.

[They obey and slowly walk away with the police.]

SCENE SEVEN

[Jesus is preaching, ringing the bell.]

JESUS
"I am the way and the truth and the life. No one comes to the Father except through Me,"

[He says this repeatedly. Clara walks up to him, listens to Him for a while then asks him ...]

CLARA
"Lord, Moses saw God face to face, show me the Father, and that will be enough for me."

JESUS
"Clara, I have been with you all this time, and still, you do not know Me? Anyone who has seen Me has seen the Father. How can you say, 'Show me the Father'? Do you not believe that I am in the Father and the Father is in Me? The words I say to you, I do not speak on my own. Instead, it is the Father dwelling in Me, performing His works. Believe Me, I am in the Father and the Father is in Me or at least believe on account of the works themselves.

CLARA
I believe, Lord. Yes, I believe.

[Police officers come in to arrest Jesus.]

POLICE OFFICER 1
Yes, caught red-handed! You are under arrest, sir.

CLARA
Who?

POLICE OFFICER 2
Mr. Jesus is under arrest.

CLARA
But you cannot arrest Him! He has done nothing criminal.

POLICE OFFICER 1
We'll let the court be the judge of that.

[Jesus reaches out His hands and lets the police cuff him.]

CLARA
So, you'll just let them arrest you, Jesus? No, you guys can't do that! He's not an ordinary man, you shouldn't arrest him.

[They take Jesus away with Clara talking and following them.]

Scene Eight

[Three crosses, Jack on the left, Victor on the right, Jesus in the middle.]

VICTOR

Jack, if you had not called me that day, I would not have been here today.

JACK

What? If we had made tens of thousands of dollars the night I called, you would thank me.

VICTOR

But we didn't, and we are here because of you.

JACK

Now you blame me? When we made money, you thanked me. Now this … this blame. I'm so done with you!

VICTOR

[Laughs]

Done with me, really? You think you're getting off this cross alive? You must be out of your mind.

JACK

No, I'm not. Maybe the quiet man can help us.

69

VICTOR

Who? Him? Jack! Are you insane? Is he not the same man who calls himself Messiah and cannot save himself?
[Mimics]
"I am the truth and the life" nonsense!

JACK

Boy, you are rude. "Don't you fear God, you are being sentenced with him. We are being punished justly, but this man has done nothing wrong."

VICTOR

Didn't he say he came to die for humanity's sins? Good thing I didn't believe in Him. I knew He was lying the moment my mom died in that gruesome car crash. She was too religious to have died such an excruciating death.
[Scoffs]
I don't know how that is possible. A man like me is here to die for me? Rubbish, He can't even save himself.

JACK

Shut up and stop being disrespectful. Your mom's death does not change who He is. You should be remorseful. God knows I am sorry for all of my actions that led me here today. "Please Jesus, remember me when you come into your kingdom?"

JESUS

"Truly I tell you, today you will be with me in paradise."

70

[And Jesus utters a loud cry and breathes his last. And the curtain of the temple is torn in two, from top to bottom.]

Scene Nine

[Voice and action taking place at the same time. Jack and Victor's bodies lay lifeless on one side of the stage. A large stone lies on the other side. Behind it is Jesus's body, mostly hidden by the stone.]

VOICE
Suddenly there was a great earthquake!

[A loud sound.]

VOICE
For an angel of the Lord came down from heaven...

[Enters an angel]

VOICE
...rolled aside the stone...

[The angel performs the action of rolling away the large stone revealing Jesus' body.]

VOICE
...and sat on it."

[And Jesus arises. He walks up to the body of Jack, and he pulls him up from the grave and takes him to heaven with Him.]

SCENE TEN

[Enters Clara addressing the audience.]

CLARA

Hello everyone, thank you for your time. The play you just watched alludes to the Bible. It is in commemoration of the resurrection of Jesus, which is the Easter Story. Easter also means the defeat of death and the victory of life. There is life after death, and believing in Jesus leads us to heaven.

The book of John Chapter 14, Matthew Chapter 27, and Luke 24 are some Bible passages referenced in our short play.

We have come to the end of our play. I wrote it without believing it was worth staging. A big thank you to you, our audience, everyone who took part in the success, especially my friend, Victor, who played the role of Victor. He didn't leave any stone unturned until it was staged today. Thank you all for watching. We truly hope that you have been blessed.

[Audience applauds]

[CURTAIN]

THE END

www.ingramcontent.com/pod-product-compliance
Lightning Source LLC
Chambersburg PA
CBHW051551120626

46551CB00013B/1462